FINGE
For Rainy Days 'S'

Rhymes, Songs and Games for Simple Fun with Little Children

Eileen Mc Aree

Fingerplays for Rainy Days

Table Of Contents

Introduction

Before there were parenting manuals, before there were tumble classes or baby learning videos, before we even knew the importance of early childhood learning, mothers played with their children. Finger plays, songs and nursery rhymes are a traditional way of playing with, teaching and enjoying your child. They are something you can enjoy together for free, games that can fill long minutes of waiting at doctor's offices or long car trips. Taking a child in your lap and playing simple games is a wonderful way of bonding with your child while passing on traditional songs that perhaps your own mother sang to you. Our grandmothers and great grandmothers were teaching their children counting, sound discrimination, rhyme and rhythm, mental imagery and developing motor skills. Most of all they were having fun! In a world filled with parenting blogs, enrichment programs and preschool skills workbooks, raising a small child can seem a little intense. Rhyming, chanting and singing with your child is a great way to unplug and simply have fun with your little one. This book provides an overview of many of the traditional rhymes that have been passed down over the generations. Add your own family's games to the mix.

In addition to this collection of children's favorite songs and rhymes, you will find crafts and activities that you can play at a moment's notice with little to no preparation time. Many parents are not what they would consider "crafty" and this book was written for them. All the activities listed here can be done with regular supplies most people keep in their homes every day. The object is having simple fun with your child. Sometimes the easiest crafts and projects are the most fun for tots and they are definitely the most fun for parents! Relax, unwind and prepare to get silly. Children pass through "the magic years" all too quickly. Enjoy!

Fingerplays

Fingerplays are some of the first games we play with our babies. Games like "Peekaboo!" and "How big is Baby?" provide some of the first play interactions we have with our children. No one needed to tell us to play these games. They are handed down from generation to generation because of the pleasure both parent and child receive from playing them. As you child grows a little older, there are many simple fingerplays you can play with them that will teach them about rhythm, language development and motor skills. Developmental benefits aside, the real reason to play them is to continue building that loving bond with your little one through play. Sometimes life is busy, and fingerplays are a great way to interact with your child at home or on the go. Look through the following rhymes and pick out your favorites. They might be the same ones your mother played with you!

Baby Shark

Baby Shark, doot doot, doot doot *(Take pointer and thumb and tap together in rhythm as you repeat phrase)*

Baby Shark, doot doot, doot doot,

Baby Shark, doot doot, doot doot,

Baby Shark, doot doot, doot doot,

Brother Shark, doot doot, doot doot, (Take all four fingers of one hand and tap in rhythm against thumb as you repeat phrase 3 more times).

Mama Shark, doot doot, doot doot, *(Take two hands and clap together, as if hinged at wrist. Repeat in rhythm3 more times)*

Daddy Shark, doot doot, doot doot *(Take both arms and clap together in a "v" shape in front of you. Repeat in rhythm of the rhyme 3 more times.)*

Now we swim, doot doot, doot doot, *(Pantomime swimming arms as you repeat phrase 3 more times in rhythm to the rhyme.)*

Chomp! *(End the rhyme with a CHOMP- a gentle grab on your child's arm, leg or wherever makes them giggle!)*

Bate, Bate Chocolate

Bate, bate, chocolate

Tu nariz de cacahuate

Uno, dos tres, CHO!

Uno,dos, tres, CO!

Uno dos tres CA!

Uno, dos tres, LA!

Uno, dos, tres, TE!

Bate, bate, chocolate!

Stir, stir, stir the chocolate

Your nose is a peanut!

One, two three, CHO!

One, two, three, CO!

One, two, Three, LA!

One two, three, TE

Choo Choo

This is a very simple rhyme to play with a baby or a young train lover!

Choo choo choo choo *(Tap hand in rhythm with the rhyme up the child's arm.)*

Up the railroad track

Choo choo, choo choo *(Tap your hand back down the child's arm.)*

Then it comes right back!

Come A Look A See!

This rhyme can be changed to personalize the members of your own family.

Come a look a see, here's my Mom, *(Hold up thumb.)*

Come a look a see, here's my Dad, *(Hold up pointer finger.)*

Come a look a see, Brother Tall, *(Hold up third finger.)*

Sister, baby, I love them all! *(As you name family member, extend last two fingers.)*

Criss Cross Applesauce

This is a great one for when your child has to be seated on lap for any length of time, and can make "waiting time" into fun time!

Criss, cross, applesauce *(Draw an "X" on your child's back with your finger.)*

Spiders crawling up your back! *(Tickle your fingertips up your child's back.)*

Cool breeze, *(Blow on their neck.)*

Tight squeeze, *(Give a big hug.)*

Now you've got the giggles! *(Tickle!)*

Diez Dedos

Hold up one finger every time you count another dedo, which means "finger" in Spanish. "Deditos" are "little fingers". It is fun to turn this one into a tongue twister, repeating it faster and faster each time.

Uno dedo

Dos dedos

Tres deditos,

Cuatro dedos,

Cinco dedos,

Seis deditos

Siete dedos,

Ocho dedos

Nueve deditos

Deiz dedos en los manos!

Eensy Weensy Spider

The eensy weensy spider went up the water spout. *(Pinch the thumb and forefinger of each hand, put together and twist to pantomime the spider going up, up, up.)*

Down came the rain and washed the spider out! *(Use both hands and wiggle fingers down to show the rain falling, then pull both arms apart to show the spider being washed away.)*

Out came the sun and dried up all the rain.
(Gently raise arms and let them fall to both sides)

Then the eensy, weensy spider climbed up the spout again. *(Repeat action of the spider climbing up the spout.)*

Good old Spider! He never gives up...

Five Elephants

This is a translation of a traditional Mexican rhyme. Children love the silliness of the idea of an elephant playing on a spider's web.

One elephant went out to play,

Upon a spider's web one day. *(Stretch pinched fingers apart to illustrate web.)*

He had such enormous fun, *(Hold arms wide.)*

He told another elephant to come. *(Wave hand as if motioning to come over.)*

Two elephant's went out to play

Upon a spider's web one day.

They had such enormous fun,

They told another elephant to come.

Continue rhyme through, 3, 4 and 5.

Soon that spider came right back

And saw his web about to crack.

He said, "Hey there elephants, this is no place
to play!" *(Wag finger.)*

So all the elephants went away.

Finger Family

Here is another family finger play. You can substitute the names of
family members that are important to your child.

Father finger, Father finger, Where are you?
(Hold up the first finger of one hand.)

Here I am! Here I am! *(Hold the same finger of
the opposite hand up as well.)*

How do you do? *(Make both fingers "bow" to
each other.)*

Mother finger, Mother finger, where are you?
(Hold up the second finger on one hand.)

Here I am! Here I am! *(Hold up the second finger
of the opposite hand.)*

How do you do? *(Make both fingers "bow" to
each other.)*

Continue the rhyme through the remaining fingers of your hand. You can use brother, sister, baby, or whomever is part of your own family.

Five Little Ducks

Five little ducks went out one day, *(Hold up five fingers.)*

Over the hills and far away, *(Move hand up and down like waves.)*

Mother duck said, "Quack! Quack! Quack!" *(Move fingers to mime quacking.)*

But only four little ducks came back.

Repeat rhyme through four, three, two, one, none....then begin...

Sad mother duck went out one day,

Over the hills and far away, *(Move hand up and down.)*

Mother Duck said, "Quack! Quack! Quack! Quack!" *(Move fingers to mime quacking.)*

And all of the five little ducks came back!

Five Little Mice

Your grandmother might remember this traditional American rhyme.

Five little mice on the pantry floor, *(Hold up five fingers.)*

Searching for breadcrumbs, or something more. *(Hold hand flat over eyes as if searching.)*

Five little mice on a shelf so high, *(Hold arm up with hand flat like a shelf.)*

Dining so daintily on some pie. *(With hands to mouth, mimic eating.)*

When along come the eyes of the wise old cat, *(Hold fingers in circles over your eyes.)*

Sees what those five mice are at! *(Wiggle your finger back and forth.)*

Quickly he jumps! *(Make a pouncing movement with your arms.)*

But the mice run away, *(Make scurrying movements with your fingers.)*

To hide in their little round holes all day. *(Make a circle with both hands.)*

Now, searching for breadcrumbs is very, very nice, *(Smile and nod.)*

But home is the place for five little mice *(Give your child a big hug!)*

Five Little Pumpkins

October is a fun time of year for teaching little ones this rhyme.

Five little pumpkins sitting on a gate,

The first one said, "Oh my! It's getting late!"
(Stretch and yawn.)

The second one said, "There are witches in the air!" *(Squeeze yourself like you are afraid.)*

The third one said, "Well, we don't care!"
(Wave your hand as if you don't care.)

The fourth one said, "Let's run and run and run!" *(Pump your arms like you are running.)*

The fifth one said, "I am ready for some fun!"
(Throw your arms up in the air.)

Then WHOOSH went the wind *(Swing your arms as if the wind was blowing.)*

And OUT went the light *(Clap your hands together as you say the word "out".)*

And five little pumpkins rolled out of sight! *(Roll your arms over each other.)*

Grandma's Glasses

These are Grandma's glasses. *(Circle eyes with thumb and forefinger.)*

This is Grandma's hat. *(Use hands to form a hat.)*

This is how she folds her hands

And puts them in her lap. *(Fold hands in lap.)*

Here is the Beehive

Here is the beehive, but where are the bees?
(Outstretch your closed fist, face down.)

Hidden away where no one can see!

Watch as they slowly come out of the hive...

One, two, three, four...five! *(Slowly extend your fingers as you count, reaching for a tickle when you get to five.)*

Here is the Church

Here is the church. *(Clasp hands together with fingers interwoven inside hands.)*

Here is the steeple. *(Extend pinkies together in a triangle shape.)*

Open the doors. *(Swing thumbs away from hands.)*

Here are the people! *(Flip hands upside down and wiggle exposed fingers.)*

Little Train

The little train went up the track *(run hand up child's arm).*

It went toot, toot

And then came back.

The other train went up the track *(run fingers up the child's other arm)*

It went toot, toot

And then came back.

My Little Hands

I have two little hands and they both belong to me.

I can make them do things, would you like to see?

I can shut them up tight.

I can open them wide.

I can put them together.

I can make them both hide.

I can make them jump high.

I can hold them down low.

I can put them in my lap and fold them just so.

(Follow hand motions as described.)

No, I Won't Go to Macy's

This song was originally a hand clapping song that your child's grandparents may recall.

No, I won't go to Macy's any more, more more!
(Wag finger back and forth.)

There's a big tall policeman at the door, door,
door! *(Hold arms out like you have huge muscles.)*

He grabbed me by the collar and he made me
pay a dollar

So I won't go to Macy's any more, more, more!
(Wag finger back and forth.)

Open, Shut Them

Open, shut them, open, shut them, *(Hold hand
up and facing out as you up and shut them.)*

Give a little clap! *(Clap hands.)*

Open shut them, open, shut them, *(Repeat
opening and shutting hands as above.)*

Lay them in your lap! *(Lay hands in your lap.)*

Creep them, creep them, creep them, creep
them, *(Walk your fingers up p to your chin.)*

Right up to your chin!

Open up your little mouth, *(Open your mouth.)*

But do not let them in! *(Quickly hide your hands
behind your back.)*

Pon, Pon

This is a simple traditional Spanish fingerplay. Little ones love it because they can do it themselves quite easily.

Pon, pon, nena pon, *(Tap your index finger against your palm as you recite rhyme.)*

El dedito en el pilón.

Pon, pon, nena pon.

El dinerito en el bolsón

Translation: Little one, put, put put, your little finger in the pestle, Little one, put, put your little coins in your little bag. Change the word "nena" to "nene "if you are playing with a boy.

Round and Round the Garden

This is a sure fire way to get a giggle out of a toddler!

Round and round the garden, *(Run your finger in a circle around the child's belly.)*

Goes the teddy bear.

One step, *(Begin walking fingers up the child's arm.)*

Two steps,

Tickle you under there! *(Give a little tickle under child's arm.)*

This Little Piggie

This song plays with toes instead of fingers. Hold or touch a toe of your child's foot as you count each little piggy. When you get to the last little piggy who runs home, run your fingers away from the child's foot, all the way up to their head. Lots of fun for ticklish little ones!

This little piggy went to market,

This little piggy came home,

This little piggy had roast beef,

And this little piggy had none,

And this little piggy ran, "Whee, whee, wheee"....all the way home!

Twinkle, Twinkle, Little Star

Twinkle, twinkle, little star, *(Use both hands to pulse your fingers like the twinkling stars.)*

How I wonder what you are!

Up above the world so high, *(Raise your arms up above your head and gently drop.)*

Like a diamond in the sky! *(Make your two hands form a diamond shape.)*

Twinkle, twinkle, little star, *(Repeat twinkling movements with your hands.)*

How I wonder what you are!

Slowly, Slowly

This rhyme has an alternate use: to help you get a toddler or small child moving! Trying to walk somewhere and your little one won't cooperate? Hold hands and recite the rhyme as you first walk slowly and then quickly in time with the rhyme. It will get the forward momentum going without resorting to nagging or carrying!

Slowly, slowly, very slowly goes the garden snail. *(Slowly walk your fingers up your child's arm.)*

Slowly, slowly, very slowly up the garden trail.

Quickly, quickly, very quickly runs the little mouse! *(Quickly run your hand up over the child as if a little mouse was scurrying over them.)*

Quickly, quickly, very quickly to his little house!

Skinnamarink

Skinnamarinky dinky dink, *(Hold one arm up, bent at the elbow and wiggle fingers while your other arm is across your chest and fingers touching your elbow.)*

Skinnamarinky doo, *(Switch arm positions and wiggle the fingers on your other hand.)*

I... *(Point to your eye.)*

Love... *(Cross your arms over your chest.)*

You! *(Point to your child.)*

Skinnamarinky dinky dink, *(Hold one arm up, bent at the elbow and wiggle fingers while your other arm is across your chest and fingers touching your elbow.)*

Skinnamarinky doo, *(Switch arm positions and wiggle the fingers on your other hand.)*

I... *(Point to your eye.)*

Love... *(Cross your arms over your chest.)*

You! *(Point to your child.)*

I love you in the morning, *(Bring arms up over-head make a circle with both hands.)*

And in the afternoon. *(Bring circle in front of your chest.)*

I love you in the evening, underneath the moon! *(Put your two hands together underneath the side of your face, as if going to sleep.)*

Skinnamarinky dinky dink, *(Hold one arm up, bent at the elbow and wiggle fingers while your other arm is across your chest and fingers touching your elbow.)*

Skinnamarinky doo, *(Switch arm positions and wiggle the fingers on your other hand.)*

I... *(Point to your eye.)*

Love... *(Cross your arms over your chest.)*

You! (Point to your child.)

Two Fat Sausages

Two fat sausages, sizzling in the pan. *(Tap two fingers on your palm.)*

One went POP! *(Make a popping sound with your lips.)*

The other went BAM! *(Clap both hands together.)*

Two Little Blackbirds

Two little blackbirds sitting on a wall. *(Hold up the pointer finger of each hand.)*

One named Peter, *(Bend one of your pointers up and down.)*

The other named Paul. *(Bend other pointer finger up and down.)*

Fly away Peter! *(Wiggle fingers of one hand to mimic a bird flying away and hide behind your back.)*

Fly away Paul! *(Wiggle fingers of other hand and hide behind your back.)*

Come back Peter! *(Bring hand back in front of you with pointer up.)*

Come back Paul! *(Bring other hand back to the center, with pointer up.)*

Way Up High in the Apple Tree

Way up high in the apple tree, *(Hold hands up in the air.)*

Two little apples smiled at me. *(Point to your smile.)*

I shook that tree as hard as I could. *(Pretend to shake a tree.)*

MMMM! Those apples were good! *(Rub your belly.)*

Where is Thumbkin?

Where is Thumbkin? *(Pull hand out in front of you with thumb extended, facing in.)*

Where is Thumbkin? *(Pull other hand out in front of you with thumb extended, facing in.)*

Here I am! Here I am! *(Bend each thumb as if they were talking to one another.)*

How are you today sir? *(Bend one thumb.)*

Very well, I thank you. *(Bend other thumb.)*

Run away. Run away. *(One at a time, hide hands behind your back.)*

Where is Pointer? *(Pull hand out in front of you with pointer extended, facing in.)*

Where is Pointer? *(Pull other hand out in front of you with pointer extended, facing in.)*

Here I am! Here I am! *(Bend each pointer as if they were talking to one another.)*

How are you today sir? *(Bend one pointer.)*

Very well, I thank you. *(Bend other pointer.)*

Run away. Run away. *(One at a time, hide hands behind your back.)*

Repeat the rhyme with the rest of your fingers in this order: Tall Man, Ring Man, Pinky

Action Rhymes

Step up the action a notch from fingerplays and you have action songs. What a great way to entertain a wriggling toddler! The following songs incorporate rhythm and movement perfectly so that children can develop language, humor and sequencing skills. But they won't know that...they just think they are having fun! If you have forgotten the tune to any of these classics, you can access most of them online or borrow a music CD from your local library.

Can You Hop Like A Rabbit?

Can you hop like a rabbit? *(Hop.)*

Can you jump like a frog? *(Crouch down and jump.)*

Can you fly like a bird? *(Wave arms as if flying.)*

Can you fun like a dog? *(Run in place.)*

Can you walk like a duck? *(Waddle)*

Can you swim like a fish? *(Put hands together and make swimming motions.)*

Can you sit very still? *(Fold hands and sit still.)*

As still as this?

Choo Choo Train

Here is the choo choo train. *(Bend elbows at sides and move them forwards and back.)*

Driving down the track! *(Keep moving elbows at sides while walking forward.)*

Now it's going forward. *(Keep moving elbows at sides while walking forward.)*

Now it's going back. *(Keep moving elbows at sides while walking backwards.)*

Now the bell is ringing, ding, ding, ding. *(Mime ringing a bell.)*

Now the whistle blows, toot, toot. *(Mime blowing a whistle.)*

What a lot of noise it makes wherever it goes! *(Cover ears.)*

Colors I See

(Repeat the main verse of this rhyme to incorporate all the colors of the rainbow. Children can have fun searching out the colors they are wearing and acting out the actions of the rhyme.).

Red, red is the color I see.

If you are wearing red then show it to me.

Stand up,

Turn around,

Show me your red and then sit down!

Eighty –Eight

Eighty eight around the world *(Draw a figure eight on child's back.)*

X marks the spot *(Draw an X.)*

Two big boulders *(Bump your fist twice upon their back.)*

Two tiny mice, *(Put index fingers on their back.)*

Spiders crawling up your back, *(Run your fingers up their back.)*

They bite you, they bite you *(Pinch their shoulders gently.)*

One cool breeze, *(Blow on their neck.)*

One tight squeeze *(Give a hug.)*

Now you've got the chills! *(Run your fingers down their arms.)*

Firetruck

Firetruck, firetruck, *(Mime driving a steering wheel.)*

Zoom, zoom, zoom

We'll be there soon!

Firetruck, firetruck

Zoom, zoom, zoom,

We'll be there soon!

Climb the ladder with the hose. *(Mime climbing.)*

Spray the water, out it goes. *(Mime spraying water.)*

Climb the ladder with the hose.

Spray the water, out it goes.

Ding, ding, ding *(Pretend to ring the bell.)*

Firetruck, firetruck, *(Mime driving the truck.)*

Zoom, zoom, zoom,

We'll be there soon!

Furry Squirrel

Whisky, frisky, hippity hop! *(Hop like a squirrel.)*

Up he climbs to the tree top! *(Mime climbing up.)*

Whirly, swirly, round and round, *(Wave arm around and around.)*

Down he scampers to the ground!

Furly, curly, what a tail!

Tall as a feather, *(Hold arms up high.)*

Broad as a sail! *(Hold arms wide apart.)*

Where's his supper?

In the shell.

Snappity, crackity, *(Snap fingers.)*

Out it fell! *(Open hands, palm up.)*

Head, Shoulders. Knees and Toes

Head, Shoulders, Knees and Toes

Knees and toes

Head, shoulders, knees and toes,

Knees and toes

And eyes and ears and mouth and nose,

Head, shoulders, knees and toes!

(Touch, each part of the body as you sing the song. After each verse sing it again faster. Keep going till you can't go any faster!)

Hello, My Name is Joe

This is a traditional camp song that is predictable and fun for kids big and small.

Hello. My name is Joe.

I work in a button factory.

I have a house and a dog and family.

One day, my boss comes up to me and says,

"Hey, Joe! Are you busy?" I said, "No."

Then turn the button with your left hand."

Hello. My name is Joe.

I work in a button factory.

I have a house and a dog and family.

One day, my boss comes up to me and says,

"Hey, Joe! Are you busy?" I said, "No."

Then turn the button with your right hand."

Song continues on in this way until children are using their right hand, left hand, right foot, left foot, and head. Then sing the final verse:

Hello. My name is Joe.

I work in a button factory.

I have a house and a dog and family.

One day, my boss comes up to me and says,

"Hey, Joe! Are you busy?" I said, "YES!"

Here We Go

Here we go up, up, up, *(Stand and raise arms high.)*

Here we go down, down, down. *(Lower hands and crouch down.)*

Here we go forward, *(Stand and take a step forward.)*

Here we go back, *(Take a step back.)*

Here we go round and round. *(Turn around in a circle.)*

Hokey Pokey

Repeat this verse, substituting different parts of the body in order: left arm, right leg, left leg, etc. Typically, you end the song by putting "your whole self "in and shaking all about!

You put your right arm in, *(Hold right arm in front of yourself.)*

You take your right arm out, *(Pull right arm behind you.)*

You put your right arm in and you shake it all about! *(Put right arm in and shake it.)*

You do the Hokey Pokey and you turn yourself about. *(Point your fingers up in the air as you turn in a circle.)*

That's what it's all about!

If You're Happy and You Know It

If you're happy and you know it clap your hands

If you're happy and you know it clap your hands

If you're happy and you know it and you really want to show it,

If you're happy and you know it, clap your hands!

If you're happy and you know it, stamp your feet

If you're happy and you know it, stamp your feet.

If you're happy and you know it and you really want to show it,

If you're happy and you know it, stamp your feet!

(Continue song in this pattern, substituting the phrases: Yell hooray, Jump up high, and act out corresponding actions.)

I'm A Little Teapot

I'm a little teapot, short and stout

Here is my handle, *(Put hand on hip and bend elbow.)*

Here is my spout. *(Hold your other arm straight out.)*

When I get all steamed up, hear me shout,

"Just tip me over and pour me out!" *(Bend over at the side as if pouring.)*

Jack-in-the-Box

Jack in the box, oh so still... *(Child crouches low.)*

Won't you come out?

Yes I will! *(Child jumps up.)*

Johnny Works With One Hammer

Johnny works with one hammer, one hammer, one hammer. *(Pound one fist.)*

Johnny works with one hammer all day long.

Johnny works with two hammers, two hammers, two hammers. *(Pound two fists.)*

Johnny works with two hammers all day long.

Johnny works with three hammers, three hammers, three hammers. *(Pound two fists and stamp one foot.)*

Johnny works with three hammers all day long.

Johnny works with four hammers, four hammers, four hammers. *(Pound two fists and stamp two feet.)*

Johnny works with four hammers all day long.

Johnny works with five hammers, five hammers, five hammers. *(Pound fists, stamp feet and nod head.)*

Johnny works with five hammers and then he goes to sleep. *(Mime going to sleep.)*

London Bridge

To turn this traditional song into an action rhyme, you need three or more people. Hold hands with one person and hold your arms up. The other children can walk under your arms as you sing the verses of the rhyme. At any time, you can insert the last verse, "Take the key and lock it up". Lower your arms together with your partner and "trap" a child in your linked arms. Swing your arms back and forth as you sing the rest of the verse. Then the caught child can have a turn being the "bridge" and the other kids can continue playing and singing.

London Bridge is falling down, falling down, falling down.

London Bridge is falling down, my fair lady.

Build it up with wood and clay, wood and clay, wood and clay.

Build it up with wood and clay, my fair lady.

Wood and Clay will wash away, wash away, wash away.

Wood and clay will wash away, my fair lady.

Build it up with iron and steel, iron and steel, iron and steel.

Build it up with iron and steel, my fair lady.

Iron and steel will bend and bow, bend and bow, bend and bow.

Iron and steel will bend and bow, my fair lady.

Build it up with silver and gold, silver and gold, silver and gold.

Build it up with silver and gold, my fair lady.

Silver and gold will be stolen away, stolen away, stolen away.

Silver and gold will be stolen away, my fair lady.

Take the key and lock it up, lock it up, lock it up!

Take the key and lock it up, my fair lady!

Mi Cuerpo

This Spanish traditional song may be familiar as it is often sung in Spanish and English at nursery schools. Sing it to teach body parts with repetition, movement and humor.

Mi cuerpo, mi cuerpo

Mi cuerpo hace música!

Mi cuerpo, mi cuerpo, mi cuerpo hace música!

Mis manos hacen, "pom pom pom"

Mis pies hacen, "bom bom bom!"

Mi boca hace, "la la la!"

Mi cuerpo hace, "cha cha cha!"

English translation adjusted to keep the rhythm
of the song:

My body, my body, my body makes music!

My body, my body, my body makes music!

My little hands go, "pom pom pom!"

My little feet go, "bom bom bom!"

My little mouth goes, "la la la!"

My body can go, "cha cha cha! "

Mix a Pancake

Mix a pancake, *(Make a mixing motion with
hands.)*

Stir a pancake, *(Stirring motion with hands.)*

Drop it in the pan, *(Mime dropping batter on a
pan.)*

Fry the pancake, *(Pretend to hold a frying pan.)*

Toss the pancake, *(Pretend to toss the pancake in
the pan.)*

Catch it if you can! *(Pretend to catch pancake
with pan.)*

Pop Corn

Popcorn, pocorn, sizzling in the pan *(Shake arm as if shaking a pan.)*

Shake it up, shake it up

Bam! Bam! Bam! *(Clap hands on each Bam!)*

Popcorn, popcorn, now it's getting hot! *(Shake arms as if shaking pan.)*

Shake it up! Shake it up!

Pop! Pop! Pop! *(Jump up and down.)*

Ring Around the Rosy

Ring around the rosy,

A pocket full of posy

Ashes, ashes,

We all fall down!

(Hold hands and turn in a circle as you recite this rhyme until it's time to fall down!)

The cows are in the meadow

Eating buttercups

Ashes, ashes

We all jump up!

(Crouch on the floor and mime picking flowers until it is time to jump up!)

Row Your Boat

Row, row, row your boat,

Gently down the stream

Merrily, merrily, merrily, merrily

Life is but a dream!

(Sit down facing child and clasp hands. As you sing the song, pull your child forwards and back.)

Shoo Fly

This classic is a great song to get some energy out when you are stuck inside! Make up new verses with your own movements...the sillier the better!

Chorus:

Shoo fly, don't bother me!

Shoo fly, don't bother me!

Shoo fly, don't bother me!

For I belong to somebody!

I wiggle, I wiggle, I wiggle like a wiggling worm! *(2X)*

Chorus

I jump, I jump, I jump like a green bullfrog! *(2X)*

Chorus

I march, I march, I march like a tall soldier! *(2X)*

Chorus

I stomp, I stomp, I stomp like an elephant! *(2X)*

Chorus

I creep, I creep, I creep like a ladybug! *(2X)*

Chorus

Sleeping Bunnies

See the little bunny rabbits *(Children lay down on the ground quietly.)*

Sleep till nearly noon

Shall I go and wake them

With a merry tune?

They're so still.

Are they ill?

Wake up bunnies! *(Children jump up.)*

Hop little bunnies! Hop! Hop! Hop! *(Clap your hands as the children hop.)*

Small as a Mouse

Small as a mouse, *(Crouch in a ball.)*

Wide as a bridge, *(Stretch arms wide.)*

Tall as a house, *(Stretch arms up high.)*

Straight as a pin! *(Place arms at sides and stand up tall.)*

Teddy Bear, Teddy Bear

Teddy bear, teddy bear, turn around. *(Turn around.)*

Teddy bear, teddy bear touch the ground. *(Touch the ground.)*

Teddy bear, teddy bear show you're your shoe. *(Touch shoe.)*

Teddy bear teddy bear, that will do. *(Shake finger.)*

Teddy bear, teddy bear, climb up stairs. *(Mime climbing stairs.)*

Teddy bear, teddy bear, say your prayers. *(Fold hands as if praying.)*

Teddy bear, teddy bear turn out the light, *(Mime pulling a string to turn out the light.)*

Teddy bear, teddy bear, say goodnight! *(Pretend to go to sleep.)*

Tick Tock

Tick tock goes the clock, *(Lift child up and gently swing back and forth.)*

Tick, tock, STOP! *(Put the child down on STOP.)*

Trot, Trot to Boston

Bounce your child on your lap in rhythm to this rhyme. At the end of the rhyme, gently drop them off your lap!

Trot, trot to Boston,

Trot, trot to Lynn

Watch out Baby

Or you might fall IN!

The Wheels on the Bus

The wheels on the bus go round and round,

Round and round, round and round.

The wheels on the bus go round and round,

All through the town.

The doors on the bus go open and shut,

Open and shut, open and shut.

The doors on the bus go open and shut,

All through the town.

The coins on the bus go clink, clink, clink,

Clink, clink, clink, clink, clink, clink.

The coins on the bus go clink, clink, clink,

All through the town.

The wipers on the bus go
whoosh,whoosh,whoosh,

Whoosh, whoosh,whoosh,
whoosh,whoosh,whoosh.

The wipers on the bus go
whoosh,whoosh,whoosh,

All through the town.

The horn on the bus goes beep, beep, beep,

Beep, beep, beep, beep, beep, beep.

The horn on the bus goes beep, beep, beep,

All through the town.

The driver on the bus goes, "Move on Back!",

"Move on back!", "Move on back!"

The dirver on the bus goes, "Move on back!",

All through the town.

The windows on the bus go up and down,

Up and down, up and down.

The windows on the bus go up and down,

All through the town.

The babies on the bus go wah,wah, wah,

Wah, wah,wah, wah, wah, wah,

The babies on the bus go wah, wah, wah

All though the town.

The mommies on the bus go shh, shh, shh,

Shh, shh, shh, shh, shh, shhh.

The mommies on the bus go shh, shh, shh,

All through the town.

And the wheels on the bus go round and round,

Round and round, round and round,

The wheels on the bus go round and round,

All through the town!

We're Going to Kentucky

We're going to Kentucky,

We're going to the fair,

To see the senorita with flowers in her hair!

Oh shake it baby shake it!

Shake it if you can!

Shake it like a milkshake and pour it in the pan!

Rumble to the bottom!

Rumble to the top!

And turn around and turn around until you
make a STOP!

Nursery Rhymes

There is a reason there are so many beautifully illustrated books of nursery rhymes. They introduce children to the world of literature, make believe and whimsy. They are rhythmic, silly and appeal to kids' sense of wonder. They provide an important introduction to rhyming skills, memory and sound recognition and are considered an important precursor to reading. They are fun to recite in the car, at the doctor's office or at a restaurant waiting for a table. Many you will recall from childhood, but the following pages provide an overview of some popular nursery rhymes.

All Around the Mulberry Bush

All around the mulberry bush,

The monkey chased the weasel,

The monkey thought it was all in fun,

POP! Goes the weasel!

Baa Baa Black Sheep

Baa baa black sheep,

Have you any wool?

Yes Sir, yes Sir, three bags full.

One for my master,

One for my dame,

And one for the little boy who lives down the lane.

Baa, baa black sheep,

Have you any wool?

Yes Sir, yes Sir, three bags full.

Five Green and Speckled Frogs

Five green and speckled frogs

Sat on a speckled log

Eating the most delicious bugs...yum, yum!

One jumped into the pool

Where it was nice and cool,

And there were four green speckled frogs...
glub, glub!

Four green and speckled frogs

Sat on a speckled log

Eating the most delicious bugs...yum, yum!

One jumped into the pool

Where it was nice and cool

And there were three green speckled frogs...
glub, glub!

Continue counting down until there is one more
green speckled frogs and finish the rhyme.

One green and speckled frog

Sat on a speckled log

Eating the most delicious bugs...yum, yum!

One jumped into the pool

Where it was nice and cool

Now there are no green speckled frogs...Ribbit!

Georgie Porgie

Georgie Porgie, puddin and pie

Kissed the girls and made them cry.

When the boys came out to play,

Georgie Porgie ran away!

Grand Old Duke of York

Oh the grand old duke of York,

He marched them up to the top of the hill

He had ten thousand men,

Then he marched them down again!

And when they were up they were up.

And when they were down they were down,

And when they were only halfway up they
were neither up nor down!

Hey Diddle, Diddle

Hey, Diddle, diddle,

The cat and the fiddle,

The cow jumped over the moon.

The little dog laughed to see such fun,

And the dish ran away with the spoon!

Hickory Dickory

Hickory dickory dock,

The mouse ran up the clock.

The clock struck one,

The mouse ran down.

Hickory dickory dock!

Humpty Dumpty

Humpty dumpty sat on a wall.

Humpty dumpty had a great fall.

All the king's horsemen

And all the king's men

Couldn't put humpty together again!

I See the Moon

I see the moon and the moon sees me.

God bless the moon and God bless me!

It's Raining, It's Pouring

It's raining, it's pouring

The old man is snoring.

He bumped his head

Against the bed

And couldn't get up in the morning.

Jack and Jill

Jack and Jill went up the hill

To fetch a pail of water.

Jack fell down

And broke his crown

And Jill came tumbling after.

Jack Sprat

Jack Sprat could eat no fat.

His wife could eat no lean.

And so between them both you see

They licked the platter clean!

Knick Knack Paddy Wack

This old man, he played one

He played knickknack on my thumb.

With a knick knack waddy wack

Give the dog a bone,

This old man came rolling home.

This old man, he played two.

He played knickknack on my shoe.

With a knick knack paddy wack

Give the dog a bone.

This old man came rolling home.

This old man he played three.

He played knick knack on my knee,

With a knick knack paddy wack

Give the dog a bone,

This old man came rolling home.

This old man, he played four,

He played knick knack on my door.

With a knick knack paddy wack

Give the dog a bone.

This old man came rolling home.

This old man, he played five.

He played knick knack on my hive.

With a knick knack paddy wack

Give the dog a bone.

This old man came rolling home.

*This rhyme can be continued up to ten, following
the rhyme pattern and inserting the following
phrases with their corresponding number:*

Six- on my sticks

Seven- up to heaven

Eight- on my gate

Nine- down the line

Ten- He played knick knack over again!

Little Jack Horner

Little Jack Horner

Sat on a corner

Eating his Christmas pie.

He stuck in his thumb

And pulled out a plumb

And said, "What a good boy am I!"

Little Miss Muffet

Little Miss Muffet

Sat on a tuffet

Eating her curds and whey.

Along came a spider

That sat down beside her

And frightened Miss Muffet away!

Mary Had a Little Lamb

Mary had a little lamb,

It's fleece was white as snow.

And everywhere that Mary went

The lamb was sure to go.

It followed her to school one day,

That was against the rules!

It made the children laugh and play

To see a lamb at school!

Mary, Mary, Quite Contrary

Mary, Mary, quite contrary,

How does your garden grow?

With silverbells and cockleshells

And pretty maids all in a row.

Muffin Man

Do you know the muffin man?

The muffin man, the muffin man?

DO you know the muffin man who lives on
Drury Lane?

Yes I know the muffin man.

The muffin man, the muffin man.

Yes I know the muffin man who lives on Drury
Lane!

One, Two, Three, Four, Five

One, two, three, four, five,

Once I caught a fish alive.

Six, seven, eight, nine, ten,

Then I let it go again.

Why did you let it go?

Because it bit my finger so!

Which finger did he bite?

This little one on the right.

One, Two, Buckle My Shoe

One, two, buckle my shoe,

Three, four, close the door,

Five, six, pickup sticks,

Seven, eight, lay them straight,

Nine, ten, let's do it again!

Sing a Song of Six Pence

Sing a song of six pence,

A pocket full of rye,

Four and twenty blackbirds baked in a pie

When the pie was opened, the birds began to sing,

"Wasn't that a tasty dish to set before the king?"

Star Light, Star Bright

Star light, star bright,

First star I see tonight,

I wish I may.

I wish I might,

Have the wish I wish tonight!

There Was a Little Girl

There was a little girl

And she had a little curl,

Right in the middle of her forehead.

And when she was good she was very, very good!

But when she was bad she was horrid!

There Was an Old Woman

There was an old woman who lived in a shoe.

She had so many children

She didn't know what to do!

She gave them some broth without any bread,

And kisses them all soundly

Then sent them to bed!

Three Little Kittens

Three little kittens have lost their mittens and
they began to cry,

"Oh Mother dear, see here, see here!

Our mitten's we have lost!"

"What?! Lost your mittens? You naughty kittens!

Then you shall have no pie!"

"Meow! Meow! Meow! We shall have no pie!"

Three little kittens have found their mittens
and they began to cry,

"Oh Mother dear see here, see here!

Our mittens we have found!"

"You found your mittens?! You good little kittens!

Now you shall have some pie!"

"Meow! Meow! Meow! We shall have some pie!"

Wee Willie Winkle

Wee Willie Winkle

Runs through the town

Upstairs, downstairs, in his nightgown.

Looking in the windows,

Rapping at the locks,

"Are the children all in bed,

For now it's eight o'clock!"

What Are Little Boys and Girls Made Of?

What are little boys made of?

Snips and snails and puppy dog tails.

That's what little boys are made of.

What are little girls made of?

Sugar and spice and everything nice.

That's what little girls are made of.

Silly Sing Alongs

Sometimes it is just time to laugh. Maybe your hands aren't free and your toddler is demanding your attention. Maybe the car ride is just going on for too long. Whatever the reason, silly songs are a wonderful way to relax and have fun with your child. The following songs can be used in many different situations, and are fun for older siblings as well as little tots. Pick your favorite and prepare to get goofy!

Bingo

There was a farmer, had a dog

And bingo was his name-oh!

B-I-N-G-O!

B-I-N-G-O!

B-I-N-G-O!

And Bingo was his name-oh!

There was a farmer, had a dog

And Bingo was his name-oh!

At this point in the song, start substituting a hand clap for the first letter of Bingo.

*-I-N-G-O, *-I- N-G-O, *-I-N-G-O

And Bingo was his name-oh!

In each subsequent verse, you will clap out an additional letter of the name Bingo, until at the end of the song, instead of Spelling out B-I-N-G-O, you will clap five times

Do Your Ears Hang Low?

Do your ears hand low?

Do they wobble to and fro?

Can you tie them in a knot?

Can you tie them in a Bow?

Can you throw them over your shoulder like a continental Soldier?

Do your ears hand low?

Do your ears hang high?

Can they reach up to the sky?

Do they soar above the nation with a feeling of elation?

Do your ears hand high?

Do your ears hang wide?

Do they wave from side to side?

Do they wave in the breeze with the slightest little sneeze?

Do your ears hang wide?

Do your ears fall off?

When you give a great big cough?

Do they lay their on the ground?

Or jump up at every sound?

Can you put them in your pocket just like little Davy Crockett?

Do your ears fall off?

Down By the Station

Down by the station,

Early in the morning,

See the little puffer bellies

All in a row!

See the station master

Pull the little handle.

Chug, chug! Toot, toot!

Off we go!

Home on the Range

Your little cowpokes may enjoy learning this traditional cowboy song.

Oh give me a home where the buffalo roam,

Where the deer and the antelope play,

Where seldom is heard a discouraging word,

And the skies are not cloudy all day.

Chorus Home, home on the range,

Where the deer and the antelope play,

Where seldom is heard a discouraging word,

And the skies are not cloudy all day.

It's Raining

It's raining,

It's pouring

The old man is snoring.

He bumped his head against the bed

And couldn't get up in the morning!

John Jacob Jingleheimer Schmidt

John Jacob Jingleheimer Schmidt

His name is my name too!

Whenever we go out.

The people always shout,

John Jacob Jingleheimer Schmidt!

Ta-da-da-da-da-da-da!

Little Bunny Foo Foo

Little bunny foo foo,

Hoppin through the forest,

Scoopin up the field mice

And boppin' em on the head.

Then one day came the Good Fairy.

And she said,

"Little Bunny Foo Foo, I don't like your atti-
tude!"

Scoopin' up the field mice and boppin'em on
the head!"

I'll give you three chances

Then I'll turn you into a goon!

*Repeat song from beginning, substituting 2 more
chances, then one more chance, and then sing:*

Little Bunny Foo Foo,

Hoppin through the forest,

Scoopin' up the field mice

And boppin'em on the head.

Little Bunny Foo Foo!

I gave you three chances!

Now I'll turn you into a goon!

Poof!

Oh well......hare today....goon tomorrow!

Mairzy Dotes

See if your little one can figure out the words to this tongue twisting
song.

Mairzy dotes and dozy dotes

And little lambsy divvy

A kiddle divvy too, wouldn't you?

What you are actually singing is as follows:

Mares eat oats and does eat oats

And little lambs eat ivy.

A kid'll eat ivy, too. Wouldn't you?

Oh Little Playmate

This song is traditionally sung as a hand clapping rhyme. Have fun clapping hands or just singing!

Oh little playmate,

Come out and play with me!

I'll bring my dollies three

Climb up my apple tree!

Slide down my rainbow,

Into my cellar door

And we'll be jolly friends

Forevermore! 1-2-3-4!

Oh little playmate,

I cannot play with you.

My dolly has the flu,

Boo-hoo-hoo-hoo-hoo-hoo!

Can't slide your rainbow,

Into your cellar door,

But we'll be jolly friends

Forevermore! 1-2-3-4!

Old MacDonald

Enjoy some time with your child singing this children's classic. The song can be as long or as short as you and your child like. Repeat this main phrase, filling in as many farm animals and their corresponding sounds as you can think of.

Old MacDonald had a farm.

E-I-E-I-O!

And on that farm he had a cow.

E-I-E-I-O!

With a moo-moo-here and a moo-moo there,

Here a moo, there a moo,

Everywhere a moo-moo!

Old MacDonald had a farm.

E-I-E-I-O!

On Top of Spaghetti

Sing to the tune of "On top of Old Smokey"

On top of spaghetti

All covered with cheese,

I lost my poor meatball

When somebody sneezed!

It rolled in the garden

And under a bush.

And then my poor meatball,

Was nothing but mush!

Oh Where Has My Little Dog Gone?

Oh, where, oh, where has my little dog gone?

Oh, where, oh where can he be?

With his ears cut short and his tail cut long?

Oh where, oh where is he?

Peanut Butter

Chorus:

Peanut, peanut butter, jelly!

Peanut, peanut butter, jelly!

Repeat chorus in between each verse.

First you take the peanuts and you pick 'em,
you pick 'em,

You pick 'em, pick 'em, pick 'em   *(Pretend to
pick berries.)*

Then you crush 'em, crush 'em, *(Pretend to crush something in your two hands.)*

You crush 'em, crush 'em, crush 'em

Then you spread 'em, spread 'em, *(Pretend to spread over a sandwich.)*

You spread 'em, spread 'em, spread 'em...

Then you take the berries and you pick 'em, you pick 'em,

You pick 'em, pick 'em, pick 'em

Then you crush 'em, crush 'em,

You crush 'em, crush 'em, crush 'em

Then you spread 'em, spread 'em,

You spread 'em, spread 'em, spread 'em...

Pizza Hut

Do the italicized actions every time that line is sung.

A Pizza Hut *(Make a square in the air.)*

A Pizza Hut

Kentucky Fried Chicken *(Flap your arms like a chicken.)*

And a Pizza Hut

A Pizza Hut

A Pizza Hut,

Kentucky Fried Chicken

And a Pizza Hut

McDonalds McDonalds *(Use hands to make an "M" in the air.)*

Kentucky Fried Chicken

And a Pizza Hut

Mc Donald's, Mc Donald's,

Kentucky Fried Chicken

And a Pizza Hut

Rain, Rain, Go Away

Rain, rain, go away.

Come again another day.

Little Johnny wants to play.

Rain, rain, go away.

There Were Ten in the Bed

There were ten in the bed

And the little one said,

"Roll over! Roll over!""

So they all rolled over and one fell out.

There were nine in the bed

And the little one said,

"Roll over! Roll over!"

So they all rolled over and one fell out.

Continue counting down until there is no one in
the bed...

There was no one in the bed

So no one said,

"Roll over! Roll over!"

Yankee Doodle

Yankee Doodle went to London

Riding on a pony

Stuck a feather in his hat

And called it macaroni!

Yankee Doodle Keep it up!

Yankee doodle dandy

Mind the music and the step

And with the girls be handy!

Simple Crafts for Little Hands

Using simple, easily found materials, you can have a lot of fun doing crafts with your child. There are whole books devoted to art with children, but the activities listed here were chosen for simplicity, accessibility and fun. Most likely you already own the materials needed and can do these activities even if you don't consider yourself "crafty".

Fun with Plastic Dough

You can let your child explore with dough in so many ways. You can easily make your own, or purchase inexpensive premade play dough at the toy store.

Some great ways to keep kids engaged while creating with play dough are as follows:

Pretend to cook! Children can use real or pretend cookie trays to make all sorts of pretend cookies, cakes and pies.

Make jewelry! Let your child roll the dough into thin rolled strips and make bracelets, necklaces and rings. Children can decorate their jewelry" with different colored play dough "jewels".

Create play dough people! Play dough is ideal for rolling so form snowmen like people. Let your children pinch off different pieces of colored play dough to make faces, hair, clothes and other accessories.

Healthy Choices Place Mats

1. Get some old supermarket circulars and a pair of scissors.

2. Let your child go through the circulars, finding their favorite healthy foods.

3. They can cut out the foods and then use a glus stick to glue them to a placemat sized piece of cardboard. If you like, laminate the placemat so it will last.

4. Your child can use the place mat at mealtimes.

Here's Your Letter

Want to put your junk mail to good use? Give your small child a pile of return envelopes, address labels, stickers and other things that are sent to you via junk mail. Let them make "mail", stuff the preaddressed envelopes and mail them in your own mail box. Just remember to take them out later!

I See You!

1. Take your old paper towel roll and give it to your child along with any drawing or art materials you have handy. Let them decorate their own telescope and then look out at the world through it.

2. If you can remember to save them, it easy to tape together two toilet paper rolls and use the same process to create binoculars as well.

Make Me A Rainbow

1. You will need a piece or scrap of construction paper in every color of the rainbow.

2. Precut the paper into half circles of descending size. The largest half circle will be red, followed by orange, then yellow on so forth till the smallest half circle, which is purple.

3. Give your child a glue stick and help them to glue one half circle on top of the next till they have made a rainbow.

Make Your Own Necklace

1. Go through your pantry and identify some foods that can be strung. Good examples are: large pasta like ziti or wagon wheels or cereals with a circle in the middle like fruity o's.

2. Wrap a piece of tape around the end of a piece of yarn.

3. Let your child string the items on the yarn till they have constructed their own necklace.

Making Marks with Markers

Markers are the easiest medium for children to draw with as they are vibrant and need little pressure to color beautifully. Markers come in many different colors, widths and styles.

Try one of the following activities to help your child have fun with markers:

Children can use fat markers to trace the lines in coloring books.

Take a coffee filter and let your children color it. The texture of the paper is such that the colors will bleed together to nice effect.

Mix colors. Let your child learn about the color wheel by mixing colors and seeing what new colors they can create.

Make finger puppets. Draw different colored smiley faces on children's fingers with washable markers or let them draw themselves. Let them put on a show with their fingers.

Color a paper towel, construction paper or computer paper. See how the colors look different on each piece of paper. Talk about why.

Musical Instruments

It is fairly simple to help children create their own musical instruments using everyday household items. Here are some ideas for homemade musical instruments:

Drums: Coffee cans, used oatmeal boxes and empty salt cylinders make great drums.

Shakers: Containers of varying sizes can be converted to "shakers" in moments. Take an empty tub of yogurt, butter, or box of pasta and put in some dried beans, rice or small pasta. Tape it up and you have a shaker!

Horns: Old toilet paper rolls or paper towel rolls make super horns.

Strings: String take a little bit more ingenuity to create. In order to make a sound you need a vibration. In writing this book (read: I never did this one with my own kids before!) I found you can cut up rubber bands across the top of a coffee can and they will make a sound. If your child is determined to be a guitar player, my suggestion would be to teach them air guitar!

The great thing about making musical instruments is that it is a project that can be an involved or as easy as you want. If you just got home from work and want to keep your child entertained while you prepare dinner, hand them a coffee can "drum" and let them march around the house. If you want to spend a rainy Saturday doing crafts, glue construction paper on the sides of your creations and let the kids decorate them.

Play with Shapes

1. Take several different pieces colored paper and cut them into different basic shapes (square, circle, rectangle, triangle).

2. If you want to practice cutting with your child you could draw the shapes and help them use scissors to cut them out.

3. Give your child a glue stick and some plain paper. Let them glue the shapes on the paper in different ways. Younger children will simply enjoy the novelty of the glue and the contrast of the colors. Older children can actually contruct pictures from the different shapes!

Post it Fun

1. Give your child a package of sticky notes and some crayons.

2. Little ones can scribble, slightly older children can draw pictures and children with some knowledge of writing can write messages on the sticky pads.

3. Allow your child to put their messages all over the house for you and other family members to find.

Rubbings

1. Take a piece of white paper and tape one end to a flat surface (table, floor, cookie sheet, etc.)

2. Place some flat, textured items under the paper. Great items

to try are: coins, keys, stencils, leaves or sandpaper).

3. Using the side of a crayon, show children how to gently rub the crayon back and forth to produce an image of the objects under the paper.

Snow Painting

If you live in an area that gets a lot of snow, this is a fun winter art activity for little ones.

1. Fill a spray bottle (or two) with water and a few drops of food coloring.

2. Let your child go outside and "paint" the snow.

Soap Clouds

1. Take a bar of Ivory soap and place it in your microwave.

2. Set your microwave for about a minute and a half.

3. Stand back and watch the soap grow into a big, lumpy cloud.

4. Take out your cloud and let the kids mush it up in a big bowl until it falls apart.

5. Put the remaining soap flakes in a Ziploc and save for the next few bath times!

Spaghetti Scribbles

Trying to get dinner on the table? Keep your kids busy while you assemble the meal with this quick and easy craft.

1. Once it is cooked, remove spaghetti from heat and drain. Take a few strands from the colander and put them aside in a bowl. Add a few tablespoons of cold water to the bowl to retain moisture and cool off a bit.

2. Give your child a piece of paper and the bowl of spaghetti strands. Let them make shapes and designs with the spaghetti strands on the paper. When the strands dry, they will stick to the paper!

Sticker Fun

Little hands haven't always mastered drawing figures the way they would like to, but if you teach your child to remove a sticker from its backing, even the littlest child can make a variety of art projects. You can purchase inexpensive stickers and form your own collection. Some great idea for easy projects are:

Door Signs: Give your child a paper plate and let them decorate it with stickers. Use ay. hole punch and a ribbon and let them hang it on their bedroom door.

Bookmarks: Let your child make bookmarks for his friends and family with stickers and sturdy cardboard paper cut into strips.

Treasure box: Give your child and old shoebox and let them cover it in as many stickers as they like. They can then keep their treasure in it under their bed.

Mommy and Me Pictures: What topic is your little one obsessed with lately? Dinosaurs? Sharks? Knights in shining armor? The two of you can make a terrific picture together. You draw a simple background like mountains, an ocean, a castle, whatever fits. Don't worry about your own artistic ability...it will look great to your child and they will love doing it with you. Then provide your child with stickers appropriate to your theme and let them finish off the details!

Tin Foil Balls

1. Rip off one sheet of tinfoil and hand it to the child.
2. Let the child squeeze the tinfoil into a ball.
3. Let them try to unfold the ball and lay it flat.
4. Give your child a crayon or marker and let them color over the textured surface of the tinfoil.

Watercolor Art

1. Simple water color paint sets are a great first painting experience for younger children.

2. Carefully show children how to dip their brush in the water and dip it in the paint, then brush the paint across the paper.

3. Remember to remind young children to rinse their brush each time and move the brush around the paper. Many a child has been sad when they continue to watercolor paint only one part of the paper and put a hole in it!

Water Painting

1. This is a fun art activity for a hot day. Give your child a paintbrush and a large container of water.

2. Let them "paint" designs on your front walk, sidewalk or driveway.

Waxy Yarn

1. Waxy yarn is great for creative play. There are a number of brands of waxy yarn that can be found in the craft aisle of your local toy store. Some familiar ones are WikiStix™ and Bendaroos™.

2. Waxy yarn can be maniputed to create jewelry, animals, people, shapes, letters or numbers. You can sort the yarn by color. You can have your child recreate shapes, practice the letters of their name or measure objects. Many of the kits actually have directions to create cute little animals and objects. You can stick your child's work on the fridge or on their bedroom door when they finish. Best of all, it leaves no mess (although you will need to wash hands after using it) so you can stow some in your bag for long waits at the doctor or car rides.

Fun Activities For Young Children

Sometimes you have lots of time to plan and prepare quality experiences with your child. Trips to the zoo, beach and park all add up to wonderful family memories. However, sometimes you have to squeeze fun into an already busy day. You may have to work all day and want to enjoy time with your child after dinner. Maybe you have a newborn in the house and you want to schedule some one on one time with an older sibling during the baby's nap. Perhaps your child is cranky, you are tired and you just need something easy. The following activities were designed with those moments in mind. Quick, easy and fun, with little or no supplies needed, each of the following activities can be begun on a moment's notice and wrapped up just as quickly!

ABC Search

Adapt this game to whatever developmental level is appropriate for your child's age. You can practice symbol recognition, early letter identification, name recognition or even sight word spelling.

1. On an index card, white board or small chalk board, write several letters or one single word.

2. Take magnetic alphabet letters that correspond to what you have written on the card. Hide each letter under a cup.

3. Children have to look under each cup to find the letter, put it on the fridge, and then cross it off their list. If they are trying to spell a word or their name, they can put the magnetic letters in order once they have crossed them all off.

Water Play

1. Water play is one of the sure fire ways to entertain children. A wise woman once said, "If you have a little crab, put it in water." Truer words were never spoken! If you are hours away from bath time and can't get to a pool, a simple dishwashing pan or bucket set on the floor can provide lots of fun for your little one.

2. Give your child lots of spoons and containers of varying sizes. They can pour water from container to container, stir, use their imagination to pretend they are cooking dinner or mixing up a magic brew.

3. If you have small waterproof boats, figures or vehicles, small children can create a whole imaginary world out of a bucket of water.

4. Clean sponges can be fun for a small child too. Show your child how light a dry sponge is, how heavy a wet sponge is, and how to squeeze the water out. Let them "wash" something like your kitchen cabinets.

5. Give your child a selection of rinsed stones from your backyard. Let them drop the stones in the water and observe how

the level of water rises.

6. Get out your child's plastic tea set and let them have a tea party. Little ones can fill the teapot, pour and serve the tea.

"Sand" Play

1. Another wonderful source of entertainment for children is playing in a sandbox. If you don't have a sandbox, or it is a rainy day, consider rice as an alternative to sand.

2. Using a standard sized plastic sink basin, pour in a large bag of rice. Let your child play with the rice in the same manner they would use sand: pouring it through funnels, filling cups, mixing it, building hills and them flattening them.

3. When you have finished, you can store the rice in a jumbo sized plastic storage bag or a plastic container till the next time!

Shaving Cream Creations

1. Shaving cream is inexpensive and can be really fun for kids to play with. It makes a satisfying sound as it comes out. The texture is light, fluffy and visually enticing. Children can squish it with their hands, stir it with a spoon or shape it into sculptures.

2. Use a couple drops of food coloring to let children experiment with color. Pink and blue make lavender, yellow and blue make green: kids can discover lots of ways to make new colors.

3. You can squeeze shaving cream into a bowl and let your child play right in the kitchen (remind them they can't taste it!). Or you can let your kids play with it in the bathtub, and really have fun! They can watch it float it the water, smear it on the walls, write in it, then just rinse them off when they are done.

Simon Says

1. Simon Says is a classic game that allows children to have lots of fun while practicing their listening discrimination skills. Children have to obey "Simon's" directions no matter how silly. Simon can tell children, "Simon says hop like a frog", "Simon says touch your head", "Simon says make a funny face", etc.

2. The only time children DON'T do what Simon says is when Simon forgets to preface their direction with "Simon says...". The child who goes ahead and still follows the direction is out. The last child in is Simon. If you are playing alone with your child, just alternate!

Hot and Cold

1. Take a small item and hide it somewhere in the room while your child is out of the room.

2. When your child returns and starts to search for the item, tell him he is "Cold" when he is far from the item and "Hot" when he is close to the item. Direct him towards it by telling him when he is getting "colder" or "hotter".

3. When he finds the item, let him hide it and you do the searching.

Hide and Seek

1. Even the littlest child can participate in a game of hide and seek. You can play indoors or outdoors, briefly or for quite a long time. You can even play while you get chores done, like putting away laundry!

2. Little children often hide in the same spot over and over again, so you may have to play along and continue "searching" for them.

3. Children can practice counting when it is their turn to search. The most fun of all is when you hide and your child is delighted at finding your hiding spot!

Lost at Sea

1. Pretend you are going on a boat ride. Your child can pack whatever they need, "lunch", "life jackets" (a sweater), "maps" (Magazines or hand drawn maps), "oars" (Pillows). Your bed is the boat.

2. Let your child's personality take the lead from there. You can pretend to see dolphins and seagulls, pirates, mermaids or deserted islands. You can use your oars to row away from sharks or hang on tight while you weather a storm. Your child can decide when you have reached your destination!

Superman!

1. Lay on your back with your knees bent and your shins facing the ceiling.

2. Place your child's belly on your shins and lift them up so they are laying on your legs with their arms extended.

3. Wiggle your child around as if they were flying. You can get silly and hum the theme song from Superman if you like!

Build a Fort

1. There are a number of easy ways for a young child to build a fort. For some reason, these little hideaways constructed out of household furniture are always more enticing than store bought tents and clubhouses. Save your money!

2. Use your kitchen table. Blankets thrown over your kitchen or dining room table make great forts.

3. Couch cushions are always a big hit for homemade forts. Combine the cushions, a chair or two and a few blankets and your child will have a great time constructing and setting up their fort.

4. Outdoor forts are even more fun! Let your child explore your

yard or local park. Let them locate a group of bushes they can hide behind, a big rock they can claim as their own, or even a secret space between buildings they can set up as their secret hideaway.

Blow Bubbles

1. Bubbles are a great way to pass the time with small children. Blow bubbles and let your child run around and pop them.

2. Teach a small tot their body parts by asking them, "Where do you want your bubble?" Children can respond with various body parts or you can provide them.

3. Use bubbles as a reward! Promise your child bubbles when they finish their dinner, come inside from the backyard or get into the bathtub.

4. Let your child try to blow bubbles themselves.

5. Experiment with different sized bubble wands. You can even make huge bubbles with inexpensive large bubble wands.

I Spy

1. I Spy is an easy game that even very young children can play anywhere at any time. Start each round by stating, "I spy with my little eye something....." For example: "I spy something blue" or "I spy something to eat". The guessing player proceeds to ask yes or no questions about the object till they figure out what it is.

2. Depending on the age of the child, you can make this as easy or difficult as you like. You can use functions of objects, color, size, letter it starts with, something it rhymes with or even who owns it.

Sorting Games

Learning to sort is skill that will later aid children with problem solving and mathematical skills. In the short term, sorting can be fun for kids and a great way to organize your house!

1. Many households have a jars or dish where they store spare change. If your child is old enough not to put money in their mouth, a fun game to play is sorting coins. Kids can begin to learn the values of different coins, earn about sorting and counting. They can compare sizes of different coins to decide which is less and which is more. Older children can even begin counting coins and switching out coins for other coins of the same value.

2. Do you have a junk drawer in your kitchen? Pulling out the junk drawer and letting your child sort it with you can be a fun way to pass the time at home with your child. Children love to hoke around in grownup's stuff. Give your little one categories like, "You find all the things we can write with and make a pile."

3. If you have a little boy in your house, chances are good you have an assortment of miniature cars. Help your child sort the cars by color. Even if they don't know all their colors by name yet, they will be able to visually discriminate between the different colors.

Highway Department

1. Do you have a child obsessed with cars? This is a fun way to play with cars. Take a roll of painter's tape (blue) and let your child design a highway on your floor. They can put the tape down themselves or be the boss and let you help them.

2. Their road can be as simple or complicated as they like. A toddler may enjoy running a truck over and over a simple two foot length of painters tape. A preschooler may have a blast taking their road form one room to another. The tape comes up easily from wood, tile or carpeting without sticking so as soon as they are done, just pull it right up.

Tea Time

1. Somehow, the concept of tea parties never gets old. A simple meal of water and toast is much more wonderful when presented as a tea party!

2. Consider using an actual tea set, if you have one. There is something exciting to a child about pouring tea from a grownups real tea pot. There are books written about how to throw a tea party. Your child will have lots of fun without any bells or whistles. Set the table, present the food on "special plates" and pour the "tea". If your child wants to make it fancier, follow their lead. Stuffed animal guests are optional!

Library Game

This is a fun way to give your child attention when you have to fold laundry, nurse a baby, or just need to sit down!

1. Tell your child to collect all their favorite books and arrange them on the coffee table. This is the library.

2. Once your child has the table full of books, they sit on the other side of the coffee table and pretend to be the librarian. You are the patron. You can ask the librarian questions about the books, ask for recommendations, and finally choose your books.

3. Hand the books to your child for check out. They can stamp them, pretend to scan them, whatever they like. Once you have the books in hand, the two of you can either play again or read the books together!

Nature Walk

If time and weather permits, a quick nature walk can be a quick and fun way to spend time with your little one. Think about what you can look for and talk about. Even a stroll around your backyard (or down a sidewalk in the city) could produce the following:

1. How many different kinds of leaves can we find?

2. What does the bark on the trees look like? Let's feel it.

3. Is there grass? What does a leaf of grass look like? How is it different than the leaf of a tree? Why?

4. Is it morning? Look for dew on the grass! Why is it there? Why does it go away later in the day?

5. Is it cold? Look for frost on the grass! Why is it there? Why does it go away later in the day?

6. Do you see any bugs? Which ones? Can you find their homes?

7. Are there flowers blooming? What colors are they?

8. Are there leaves on the trees? Why or why not? What colors are they? When will the leaves come back? Why?

9. Do you see any animals? Where do they live? How do they move?

10. Can you see any seeds? What plant are they from?

11. What about rocks? Can we find any? Are they big or small? Smooth or rough? One color or many colors? Why? Are they alive? Why or why not? Can we climb on them? Can we collect some and put them in our pocket?

12. Is there snow on the ground? What is snow? What is it made of? Do you see any icicles? What plants are still green when there is snow on the ground? Why?

13. What animals can you see in the cold winter months? How do you think they survive?

Laundry Basketball

Need a game to play while you fold up the laundry? Take a pair of rolled up socks and set up the laundry basket some distance away. Your little one can have fun trying to get the socks in the basket.

Depending on the age of the child, you can decide to move the basket further away every time they get it in. This can be played with a group of children, one child alone, or you can take turns with them, turning the mundane task of laundry into something a little more enjoyable!

Fun in a Minute: Emergency Supplies to Keep On Hand

There are certain items that are a good idea to keep in your house. Like a well stocked kitchen, making sure you have a few basic items can make entertaining children much easier. In addition, many of us have to work either full or part time. At other times you just need to get away for a few hours for one reason or another. If you are bringing your child to Grandma's or the babysitter, it's nice to be able to throw a few things in a bag and know your caregiver will be able to have fun with your child without resorting to TV or the computer (at least not every time!). The items that follow are inexpensive, convenient to keep in your home and easy to use. Don't worry about homemade paper mache or sewing machines required. Take a look at the following list and don't be surprised if you already own all the items. Dig in and have fun!

Music

Music tames the savage beast and entertains the most energetic child! Here is a short list of some of my favorite musical performers for children.

Jeffrey Friedberg and the Bossy Frog Band

Hands down my family favorite. Jeffrey is local to the area where I live and with children ranging from 6th grade down to Preschool, I've been listening to the Bossy Frog for a long time. I still love the original Bossy Frog CD we purchased when my sixth grader was two and we have purchased several others over the years. His lyrics are catchy, wholesome and have humor embedded for both children and adults (Check out: Something smells.....It's my nose ...) If you live in the New York metropolitan area, the band performs shows for free at most local libraries so you can check him out for yourself. CD's or digital downloads are available at www.bossyfrog.com

Hap Palmer

Hap Palmer was making music for children before I was born and his songs are as wonderful today as when they were first created. If you visit his website you will see forty years worth of musical creations. My personal favorites are the original *Learning basic Skills through Music (Vol I and II)*, *Baby Songs Soundtrack* and *Learning in Two Languages: Aprendiendo en Dos Idiomas*. Because Hap Palmer has been creating music for so many years, many of his CD's are available at local libraries. Borrow one or visit www.happalmer.com to look through his collection and pick your own favorites.

Music With Sara

By now you have probably noticed the sprinking of Spanish within this book. Learning Spanish is a continuing event at our house, but even if that is not something you are interested in, these catchy songs will have your children listening over and over. The original

Canciones en Español and *Mas Canciones en Español* contain so many fun, danceable tunes that you will be love them just for the fun factor. Songs are available as CD's or digital download at www.musicwithsara.com

Raffi

Singable Songs for the Very Young was the first children's CD I ever owned. Back when I had my first child I felt grateful to Raffi for teaching me something to sing to her! Raffi crafts fun, wholesome and catchy songs for children. A combination of original Raffi tunes and classics, the soundtrack of raising my four little ones would have been very different without songs like *Baby Beluga* and *We're Going to the Zoo*. In writing this book, I found out that he is currently advocating for children's safety online so now I love him even more. Another classic performer, his work is also available for lend at many libraries. To purchase, look through his collection at www.raffinews.com

The Laurie Berkner Band

You may recognize the voice of Laurie Berkner form children's television but it is her CD *Buzz Buzz* that I regularly use to get my own children as well as my preschool students up and moving. *I Really Love To Dance* and *Buzz Buzz* are great songs for dancing around the living room. *There's a Little Wheel that Turning in My Heart* has been turned into a bedtime song at our house. The Laurie Berkner Band has many CD's and digital downloads available for sale and you can preview them at www.laurieberkner.com

Art Supplies

If you are not a crafty person, but want to keep basic art supplies on hand refer to the following list. These supplies require minimal set up and clean-up, which means in most cases you can squeeze a fun activity in a short amount of time, pack them for travel, or allow kids to do on their own.

Drawing Supplies:

Pencils

Crayons

Markers

Papers:

Plain computer paper

Construction Paper

Coloring Books

Painting:

Watercolor Sets

Paint brushes of varying sizes

Dot Style Paint Markers

Manipulatives:

Plastic Dough

Clay

Waxy Yarn

Various Supplies:

Child size scissors

Glue

Cotton Balls

Tape (Now there is duct tape to play around with available in so many patterns and designs.)

Glitter

Games

The following games are developmentally appropriate for children under five but are still fun for older siblings to play, too. The teacher in me couldn't help but list the developmental benefits but bottom line: they are just fun!

Cards

Simple card games like Go Fish encourage symbol matching, number recognition and turn taking skills. You don't need to purchase a special set of cards, a standard set of card will work just fine. You can also try:

Big Brother: A junior version of the classic game "War", each player throws down a card. Your child has to use the numbers and pictures to figure out who has the bigger number. The "big brother" (or sister) gets to keep both cards.

Old Maid: Use one of the queens as an old maid and have fun while your child matches number to number and picture to picture.

Fly Swatter: Give your child a plastic fly swatter. Lay our several cards. Say a number and your child can swat the corresponding card. If correct, they get to keep the card. Hint: this works just as well as a multiplication or vocabulary review when they are older!

Dice

Regular dice can be used in a variety of fun ways to entertain young children. Giant foam dice are fun for little ones to roll, but standard dice available at any convenience store work just as well. Roll one die, count the dots together and decide on an action to do that many times. For example: Roll a "2" and you can jump two times, roll a "3" and bark like a dog three times, etc.

Memory

This is one game where children generally can excel and beat the adults! There are many varieties available, form the original to Memory games featuring you child's favorite character.

Candyland

Ahh..... the fantasy of visiting the land of sweets! Kids practice color recognition, turn taking, counting and sequence while trying to get to the King of Candy. Always fun for kids and adults.

Hi Ho Cherry Oh

Encourage fine motor skills, counting and subtraction and addition in this cute game.

Connect Four

Recognizing patterns, counting and problem solving are all developed while playing this two man game.

Cranium Caribou

Teach color and letter recognition through this totally fun treasure hunt game.

Guess Who?

Kids have to develop their language skills in this facial recognition game. It is a fun way to let kids look for details and practice formulating good questions.

Zingo

Preschool version of bingo promotes symbol recognition for little ones and sight word recognition in older kids. It is so simple to play that even a toddler can reasonably join in.

Made in the USA
San Bernardino, CA
18 June 2020